HUMANE INTENTIONS VOL. 1

SAMUEL DONTE DJUAN DAVIS

SIMMS BOOKS PUBLISHING

Publishers Since 2012

Published By Simms Books Publishing

Jonesboro, GA

Copyright © Samuel Donte Djuan Davis, 2017

All rights reserved. No part of this book may be reproduced, scanned, or distributed in any print or electronic form without permission. Please do not participate in or encourage piracy of copyrighted materials in violation of the author's rights. Purchase only authorized editions.

Library of Congress Cataloging in Publication Data

Samuel Donte Djuan Davis

Humane Intentions Vol. 1White Book

ISBN: 978-0-9983311-5-7

Printed in the United States of America

Edited by Mary Hoekstra

Book Arrangement by Simms Books Publishing

Cover by Urias Brown, Michael Shield Studios urias@michaelshieldstudio.com

Just wanted to acknowledge all the people who stood by me when I had nothing and who helped me get to this point:

Marlene Banks

Chester Banks

Chelsey Banks

Chester Banks Jr

David Williams

Kanisha Thomas

Mychal Davis

Tiara Malone

Marcus Warner

Marc Reeves

Dateney Ewing

Table of Contents

A Woman's Perspective

Chapter 1

When a woman loves

The mind of a battered woman

Lost your treasure (Letter 2 my Ex)

Weary eyes

Fatigue

Common situations

The afflictions of a woman in agony

Although I'm damaged, I deserve better

Loyalty

Gone

Random Emotions

Chapter 2

Angel of mines

Submission (Trust and Love)

Diamond in the rough

Stop snooping

Laziness

Even grown men cry

Lack of communication

Nothing like a loyal woman

Nobody is as real as they say

Fight for your love!!!

Take responsibility

Irate

This is ME!

Broken hearted

Devil in a red dress

Random Emotions

Chapter 2

All I need is you

What sign am I?

There are some things about women I'll never understand

The portrait of a woman

Dying other half

Humane intentions

Sinner's prayer

Soothing the mind

My women

The walls have eyes

Internal truth

Ball of confusion

Nice guys get no credit

I don't respect money

Here we go again

Strengths, Weaknesses and Life lessons

Chapter 3

Let words be words

Soldier's mentality

Success

Watch your tongue

4 Footsteps

Keep quiet

Is love enough?

The characteristics of love

So much pain

The fear of love

Embrace your human side

Words from a changed man

Tired of running

Good morning

Cherish a good woman

Strengths, Weaknesses and Life lessons

Chapter 3

Smooth operator

Be a man 2 your woman

Ladies, respect yourself

No longer blind

My love

4give me

Keep your eyes and ears open

Choices

Some things in life are simply unavoidable

Why we broke up

Mistakes

What you won't do another man will

4giveness

Real life

Chapter 4

Self-respect

Loud ones

Loner

I know my position

Still aren't satisfied

Been waiting on you 2 love me

Tired of being tired

Life is precious

Faith without works is dead

Fear

My mission

Goodbye

Blindfolded

Lies (The reason why men lie)

We are what we think

A Woman's Perspective

Chapter 1

When a woman loves...

When a woman loves she loves wholeheartedly; it stems from her soul
She would sacrifice herself to please her man, even if it seems he's doing everything he can to break her down emotionally
Far from fragile, she stands firm

Because when a woman loves, she loves not just who he is but who he could be
She exposes her vulnerability
She loves unconditionally, through the rain and the pain
When a woman loves, she'll laugh at his jokes even if they're corny
Some find it phony but she'll use all her energy to make you feel like a man just to make him happy
A woman's love is deeper, more emotional, more spiritual and abides on a mental level only real men can know

A woman's love is not to be taken for granted
She loves with a passion so powerful

A man who hasn't felt it could find it so unbelievable
Deep down she knows he may hit a curb, and she knows mistakes will occur
When a woman loves, the way a woman loves, all she craves is assurance behind her man's words

The mind of a battered woman

Headaches, broken promises, cheating, cursing and tears

describe a relationship I was in for 10 years

After he was sent to prison for dating a younger girl I felt a sense of relief

I finally realized I was a pearl

I began to pick myself up, fix myself up, still remembering my disbelief the first time he struck my face

Standing in front of a mirror, looking then through swollen eyes, I tried but could not remember just how beautiful I was

I allowed him to reduce my self-esteem

He tried to control me mentally when he

was supposed to console me

I remember still all those whores, sluts and ugly things he called me

He shoved me away when he was the one supposed to hold me

But when our self-esteem is down and out we women will let men tell us anything and believe them without question.

All the time it was him who really had the insecurities

He failed to realize he had my heart for eternity

But after being broken hearted I began to protect my feelings and with that my heart hardened

Now I'm well-guarded

Time has begun to heal all bruises and internal, invisible wounds

Once again, I beautifully bloom, I am reborn

I am pure like a newborn just out the womb

Lost Your Treasure (My Letter to My Ex)

It's over, we're through!

You made everything about you

You should have thought about me, at least a little

Now you stalk me, stall me, show up unannounced.

Now are you trying to redeem yourself?

for all the times you never called me?

You left me lonely, all for your so-called homies. I am left having to sit back and listen to you vent about how phony they are

Been waiting on you for years. Now I'm tired of talking at all. You won't address your inability to love me

What is there to say?

When I felt weak it was not a signal for you to verbally abuse or attempt to control me

I was concealing our information; you were revealing information.

I was trying to salvage and rekindle our relationship; you were lobbing bombs in chosen directions

All those times I was sad? They meant, please console me...

All those times I felt vulnerable? They meant please hold me.

But you were so unmindful then; I didn't think you would have noticed if I were gone.

Now I am.

You have at long last begun to analyze what's in my mind

You can't, I am beyond you.

Anything anybody wanted to know, they knew who to come to...

You!

You threw out advice for everyone's relationship but your own

You talked a good game; you should have listened to yourself, too.

You claiming you're a man? Man, you act like your brain is the size of your shoe

How you aspire to be the treasury of the state

but lost-your treasure?

What more did you want from me? I promised I was yours forever

How could you say you loved me?

That should have been your incentive to make things better

Before us, you had nothing.

I gave you clothes and shelter

You spent three years pursuing me; once I gave in, you chose to do whatever

You made me think I was the transgressor

When I was the one trying to put the pieces together

We lived together but you thought you could come in whenever, you thought you could expect me not to realize or improvise.

I won't tolerate that... even so I wish you well on your endeavors.

I hope you live life for the better, starting now.

Signed... Your former heart investor.

Weary Eyes

Days at a time, I wore shades, masking my eyes, denying all witnesses from spying the trembling anguish clouding my mind.

This dominion over my actions manipulated my thoughts, my sense of gravity, and left me not knowing where I was at times.

When I was an adolescent, someone close as my family and all pure trust, robbed me of my innocence. I began behaving outlandishly.

This surviving agony is one façade I have yet to abolish, because it's not a façade of fantasy, it's a wall of-reality!

Now, perhaps forever, I long for seeds for strategies to alleviate my sorrow.

Until and if that time dawns, my walls exist; they are no mirage

I'm tired of this pain, tired of these lies, tired of the rain!

Despite such distractions and behind my shades, I still clearly see my flawed family montage

Fatigue

I gave you love; you gave me lies

I gave you support without divide. I gave you trust; you breached it, giving me cunning capers and phony disguises

Secret infidelities!

I gave you loyalty; you embraced adultery

I gave you chances, leniency and far too much credit

Even with your mere words, you could've given me assurance; instead, you created and molded a mystery

You were far too preoccupied, thinking I was dumb; you failed to see my woman's intuition is, was, and will be my greatest quality

I gave you my heart; when you broke it, I became that pillar of salt, formed from so many tears, so little truth.

Heartless!

You expected me to turn a blind, teary eye on everything you taught me

I forgive you, and do so by knowing

everything will be done unto you as you've done unto me

We all reap what we sow.

I will not plant bitter seeds from your heart; I will rise to power and advantage, leaving you blind and becoming a liability

I loved you; you never saw it.

Selfishness and immaturity could not handle me as who I am, not who you wanted me to be

I walked away from loneliness, constant tears and emotional misery

I moved forward, seeking pure, unadulterated love spinning endless possibilities

Common Situations

Even though I smile and maintain my composure, everything is far from picture perfect and beneath the surface

I forgot my own; without him, life seemed worthless

He pranced around without a care in the world, seeing me as his servant

Frankly, he without me? Nobody would have his naked back.

His mother recently died from cancer and before she died I made a promise to be there when he needed me and to forever be honest

How can I maintain, if he's not putting forth effort or homage?

While I feel alone, he becomes more ignorant and unaware of my vital logic

He says he understands, he loves me but his gestures so blatantly speak otherwise

He prefers ancient topics, forcing me to discuss them, when I just want him to drop it

Ignore him?- He gets irate; he puts his hands around my neck until I can barely breathe and with a distorted voice, I scream, stop it

When his mother was alive, paying her medical bills

Left our pockets empty

Even so, he has the audacity to spend scarce currency on foolish investments rising from his irrational mind.

I never would have thought the man who claims to love me would treat me like an object

Using and abusing me then throwing me to the side like the worn old wallet in his back pocket

My friends say I have no one to blame but myself

Reality is to the contrary; the same friends are never here to help

My heart has grown jaded and numb from years of waiting for him to come around

He's nothing without his trophy. How else do you think he captured his invisible crown?

Truthfully, I exalted him; I lifted him; I raised him up.

Good women like me go unnoticed and even unseen; not me, I'm bringing it back around

The afflictions of a woman in agony

Before I got involved in this crazy relationship,

I was standing on my own two

He swept me off my feet; he was loving and affectionate for a minute.

After he got his, he started changing like most unstable men.

Although, sure, he took care of me financially

but all the agony he inflicted didn't cover his attempts at goodness

I gave this man my heart, mind and soul; I gave him my life

I loved him, so I accepted the things he said, wrong or right.

While he was out doing whatever, I was in, I stayed home, I was faithful, crying my eyes out late countless nights from this dramatic plight.

I'm an emotional wreck but my tolerance level has reached its peak

Love is blinder than blind. I gave him any sexual favors he desired; he desired to receive it from someone else's woman, some other man's wife

I took care of him, as his cook, as his housekeeper, every day and night. Dead tired I was, but when I got fed up and voiced my opinion, he cornered me; he hurt me, with his horrific acts of spite

Other men say I'm beautiful; I don't have to accept this situation, with its obvious injuries I cannot hide.

He verbally and physically abuses me. I go to work with marks and bruises on my neck and face

People stare; I'm the one afraid to walk in a public place

I'm not the type to shriek or shout when he asks for money; I give it cause I love him.

Tell me though, what type of man doesn't go out and get it on his own? How sad would it be to see if most of them have forgotten their places?

Ignorant of the truth, I tried to conceal it

While he makes me feel less of a woman, in the end, he's the one going to feel it

Him saying he's authentic around his friends,

while with me he's not man enough to reveal it

Just to hurt me, he says nobody will want me because of my stretch marks, but some of his so-called friends wink at me with subtle remarks

I can't change him; I know that; I hope he alters his ways

I refuse to take any more of his cheating; no more abusive ways.

He will have to finally put this beauty to use

because this wasn't the way I was raised

Although I'm damaged, I deserve better

My damaged heart has trust built in, and its frail.

You have the characteristics of the man of my dreams and you scare me more than going to jail.

I'm afraid to bestow my heart again; it's been broken by many disloyal men, better known as little boys, who damaged my heart like their little boys' toys

That's why, every time you ask to come around, I quickly try to avoid meeting you on uneven ground.

Show me you utterly want me!

Show me I'm more than a trophy.

See, I'm a beautiful woman of loyalty, with standards, demanding I will be treated as royalty.

See, I need companionship, but not all for me. If you accept me, you must also receive my son

We need a man, someone willing to spoil us with love, guidance and fun.

I deserve an affectionate, kind-hearted man; I refuse to endure blatant disrespect from a man who is truly a no one.

I'm no longer settling; love me for me, or you'll have none of me...

I'm longing for a man who'll let me be me and will compliment my true identity.

All that's damaged has not been destroyed; all that's me longs for a man to be free.

Loyalty

How can you be so loyal to the streets, your money, your homies, but your loyalty stops with your wife and family?

Who has held you down for years, even when you felt you lost your sanity? Who held fast when you behaved erratically?

You being ignorant that only God knows your heart, God knew only a good woman like me would help you reconnect with your elation

Blinded by your own lies

Drowning in the sea of your own vanity

I understand the sadness of your bursts of insanity

There is no justification for your insolence, your useless profanity

Already suffering undying agony of growing up without a daddy, why would you put your son through the same emotional catastrophe?

You've burdened me to cope on my own, yet you can't seem to fathom all the nagging

Some nights you don't even come home, leaving me alone, your son alone; this is pure exasperation

Indulging in secret sexual escapades, ensuring another woman's rent is paid

How can you clearly not know why aspects of your life are lacking?

God doesn't like ugly, nor is He too fond of cute.

You label yourself a grown man, when your pants are sagging

You put your trust in the streets, instead of in me.

You can't even see why your plans, like your pants, are dragging

Nothing good happens when you're doing wrong.

You've made a vow to God, who, with me, sees you steal away from our home

Gone

My love for you is the essences of our relationship, deep beyond the abyss, but now I know you must go.

I loved you without conditions; I accepted the consequences,

but now I must let you know

When you needed assistance whether money or attention,

I was there

I took good care of you while you were unemployed, sitting at home stiff as a statue

You were thinking you had no benefit to me; like the majority rules, you as the man had one mindset, to control our relationship.

You were claiming you had other things to do with it, but you were living here; this house was your first priority

You forgot we both lived here, sleeping here every night. You clearly expressed with every gesture, you're nothing but a tenant

You were trying to convince yourself you're a man, but you can't even get a grip on the basic characteristics qualifying you're a man

At the same time, you always found a way to fund your habits, no matter we were in a jam

You were paying everything else but the necessities at home

You were merely satisfying what roamed through your dome

I know no man is perfect; I know the first thing a man is supposed to do is take care where he rests his head

To reduce the stress, to feel a sense of comfort, before he lays his head down in bed

I'm settling for a heart that I no longer own.

You're not doing what you're supposed to do, I can't tolerate or condone

If I'm going to struggle, I'd rather struggle alone and survive on my own

It's sad to say, a majority of these men have forgotten their roles

Like scared lost souls, what a negative image they impose

I've given you chances after chances; but instead of keeping on, I simply want you gone

Random Emotions

Chapter 2

Angel of Mine

You instantly put your hands over your eyes,

like you just walked

down the stairway from heaven,

that's the way your beauty shines

Too much for human eyes to define,

Impeccable, like wine, innocent and divine

A walking diamond

This heavenly angel of mine

Submission (Trust and Love)

Is this what I've been running from my entire life?

Is this what my trembling heart desired, but was too afraid to act?
Must I figure it feels good, while not knowing I'm falling in love?
I'm at a point in my life where I'm willing to fall, risking it all
My heart, unguarded and open, is something I've never imagined
How comical it is in life, to think you'll never meet that right person, because of what you see...
Until you've met that imperfect person of understanding, and they modify your perspective on commitment, love, trust and maturity
You learn to actually love someone other than yourself; you realize it's trusting and contributing 100 percent, not 50
Reminiscing on the period in my life when I couldn't trust anybody, when I lived solely for myself with no babies
When I tried convincing myself I could make it, without love or assistance from anybody
Truthfully, we all need somebody or our attitudes will leave us lonely, when we really don't want to be
I've finally surrendered to love and it has sculpted me
I can boldly say my lady helped change me
When you find someone that loves you despite your flaws, keep a tight grip on them.
We all need someone to love and trust in this life, lest we call it the loveless journey

Diamond in the rough

Nowadays, having a good woman is a blessin`

Unfortunately, more than half of them are being faithful to the wrong man, who consistently cheats and hasn't learned his lesson.

A woman's worth is gold,

But her man is oblivious to the fact that his woman is his most valuable possession.

Rupturing the heart of a faithful woman however, men like me have to endure the backlash of other men's indiscretions.

It's seldom that those who had relations with several jerks quickly recognize a good and candid man with a true connection.

Initially, they wouldn't know what that was for the lack of real love and honest affection.

They wonder what is so complicated about gauging why some women are irate with men; why they nag; why they use their tongues and kids as a weapon.

I'm not justifying their actions; I'm just saying there's an understandable logic behind some of their actions.

Women are more emotional creatures who love with a passion; their love flows calm and slow like the ocean

If we were behaving more like men maybe they would think before reacting, instead of birthed off someone else's notions and emotions

STOP SNOOPING

What happened to a little privacy?

You're giving me permission to go through your things just so you can have authorization to go through mine.

I've been truly faithful but you claim you don't have a positive identity

It saddens me to conceal my phone like a gun I keep in my jeans

I still feel you digging in my pockets, the result of not trusting; I feel you up late at night, snooping through my things while I sleep

Or at least that's what you're thinking

You've expressed you've had a hard time trusting men from the beginning

I've received your venting about your previous relationships, how they hurt you and cheated; how you gave them your all; and questioning me about how they cheated, guilt free, so easily

I just didn't expect such immaturity, or you taking it to the point of no return before you flooded that void

Accusing me of these outrageous things

Literally begging to invade my phone while uttering that will bring you trust when I never even heard your phone ring

To my eyes your phone is invisible, like puppet strings

I've not indicated I'm untrustworthy

I've allowed you to accompany me and my friends

I would put my phone on speaker so you could listen to my conversations and prove I'm not killing trust

I work hard every day; I come home to you; I give you plenty green;

I carry all the weight on me; I pay all the bills, including you and your phone bill; and you don't compensate for a damn thing

How is it, when I loved you with no conditions, while being accused of having dishonest intentions

You're the one who doesn't trust me without a legitimate reason, so I should be the one thinking I need someone different

You are ignorant to the fact that you have no competition

We're not even married and you're claiming I have a mistress...

All because I won't allow you to meddle through my belongings and my business

Those are the types of actions that would cause the average man to search outside his home

I'm afraid to leave any of my valuable things with you at home, because I've walked through the door and everything I owned was everywhere, encroached upon, rummaged through, ripped up and thrown

I've been faithful and patiently waiting until you learn to trust me

I've made clear as honesty gestures that you can trust me

The entire duration of this relationship I have loved you wholeheartedly

But you're beginning to push me away all because of your own uncertainty, your lack of trust in me, and your fear of your man having even a speck of privacy

Laziness

Laziness isn't conducive to being ambitious

There's no food for a shiftless man who doesn't work and accrues his profits, making it easier to generate thoughts that are pernicious

A man should get up and work for his own, not nail down that responsibility on his woman's back

When she's your most valuable possession, she should be kept under protective custody, like a material witness, whereabouts secure

Never quitting, handling his business which should be every man's primary mission

Some men just aren't made like they used to be made

Some men used to have the necessary essentials and mental tools to tighten screws when they were loose

Now we have our woman go out and work, to compensate the bills, having no goals, no self-motivation, no ambition, and no sense of urgency to reboot

Used to be, a man doesn't work, a man doesn't eat

How can you teach order in a house where you regularly sleep, when you won't pay a bill, clean or disburse anything?

Even Grown Men Cry

I'm a human first then a man just like you…

This entitles us to concoct mistakes, have regrets, ride emotional roller coasters, and face the simple obstacles before all of us

Despite the fact that I am a man, I hurt and feel pain as severely as you do

Don't allow anyone to make you feel less of a man because you've cried.

Believe me; the guy who tries to criticize you may be dying inside;

Holding in his own emotional baggage because he's too petrified to cry

I never consider statistics or what the world's multitudes say and do

I do what I want to do

If I feel like crying, that's what I'm going to do

Our eyes are our window blinds; when the sun shines through and bares our souls, lays bare our weaknesses, and unveils key elements that do not make us whole

Weeping heals then rejuvenates our mind, body and soul, from lingering toxic trash and green-bile spleen that camouflage our egos

The masses ask me, "Are you afraid to cry?"

And I reply, "Look into the truth in my eyes."

Allow those emotional fumes to fly

Because grown men cry,

Lack of Communication

When the communication fades so does the connection expecting me to know what's on your mind when you've failed to speak your inner expressions

Closed mouths don't get fed…

If you don't unveil what's in your head,

you can't expect me to see thoughts left unsaid

Knowing you for several years, I understand I should know certain things sometimes

Honestly, I don't want to have to figure out what's on your mind. I don't want to watch your crazed facial expressions, subliminal inclinations or watch the way you blink for some cue

When you could just say what you're thinking

Accost me with directness; this lack of communication floods and drowns our relationship

I cannot know what's on your mind if you don't speak directly

If you want things to change, begin with boldly expressing yourself

Because you reveal your spleen towards me

when things don't proceed accordingly

While what you needed to tell me, you never said

You hide things you should have shown me

Remember closed mouths never get fed and you'll find yourself by yourself, extremely hungry

Nothing like a loyal woman

There's nothing more appealing than a loyal woman,

Loyal not just through good times but also through intense discord and life's sudden disruptions

Fighting with you and for you though sticking by your side when you've had enough or nothing of me

Never judged or disparaged you, when you wept

Stood strong for you when you were spiritually weak

Didn't run home to her parents when you said we might have to live on the street

Encouraging you, defining a disadvantage we will defeat

She represents a tree with roots planted with mine

A strong, honest woman of understanding

If your lady has been there for you when you could barely make ends meet
Make sure she yearns for nothing when you get on your feet

NOBODY is as real as they say

Let's be straight!

NOBODY is as real as they say

Regardless of the perfect picture we attempt to paint or the stories we narrate

We're all humans entitled to render mistakes or perhaps procrastinate

Our human ways and the words we convey...

Do not always copy the gestures we make

We're conceived in sin; we've developed sinful ways

yet that's not a mental state we always have to illustrate

One of the criteria of being real is not only uttering what you feel,

but also making clear that every thought we think isn't meant to articulate

We wonder why somethings we want to do never go as planned,

We're always having to delay

For everything has a time and place

Nobody's as real as they portray

Fight for your love!!!

What's love without tragedy?
What's a relationship without trust?
Don't let your pure pride lead you blind, cause you to tarnish shared love because you can't overlook the rumors and allegations

If you truly love your mate do what you must to keep that love
What happened to fighting for your love?
These days, people mistake love for infatuation, sex, and sin
That's why it's so easy for them to let it end
No relationship will be perfect, but for those who deserve it, make it mend

I understand in certain situations it isn't worth harboring in the end

What's the point of love if you're not willing to make amends?

Take responsibility

Ladies, I know you might be enthused by attractive lies from a man's lips and eyes

Don't give that guy all your power because he declares what is his is ours

Although you were designed to submit, submit only to a man whose words and his actions are in line

Some of these guys are plastic…

When you begin dating or begin a relationship, listen and pay attention

Don't be timid trying to speed up the situation

Let it flow because you know sometimes things don't go the way you hoped…

Don't denounce all men when YOU didn't make a full evaluation

Don't point the finger

Own the responsibility for the anguish you-accept and the actions you're makin'

You speeding the situation with sex caused his true colors to awaken

Irate

No heart, No love, No emotions

How can I have an active heart when it is frozen?

How can someone say they love you when they're the reason for your heart's corrosion?

Apologizing won't suffice

A broken heart combined with love is a recipe for two hearts' ice

My heart exploded into millions of pieces, was mercilessly ripped from stark ignited passion of eye contact between my lady and a guy she said she met at a park

Stating vengeance is mines!

She heard the rumors I was being unfaithful and you believed it

Instead of approaching me like an adult to salvage some time

You showed your heart is so unkind

You presume instead of asking me, then go back to nagging every time I want to relax and unwind

If you needed anything I had, I assured you I'd give you mine

My actions spoke directly to you those where my signs

I made sure you were ok, but whatever you had going on, you didn't have it in line

You actually fixed your mouth to utter allegations that you've surmised

When you've been implementing your own sexual escapades that you've secretly contrived

Thinking I'm unable to see through your sly disguise

My vision is far beyond a normal human's optics I can see into your family's future's lives

Accumulating all the pain until I erupt causing major damage like when the lava from two volcanoes collide

This is me!

I'm authentic, I don't talk much. I don't have many friends since I'm preoccupied creating power moves

I don't follow man; man will lead you astray

I make my own crowd, my own rules, my own way

I work to elevate, investing to cover my dues

When there's a problem I fix it, I carry my own tools

I'm cool but not that cool, been known to be a tad bit rude

because I don't fraternize with ignorant dudes

I socialize with a certain group of guys

The real to be exact, if you don't embody growth and development, I'll quickly fall back

I don't associate myself with too many folks, most are fake

I walk alone to abbreviate the hate

The more friends you derive, the more your name will carry weight

The more you converse with snakes, the more likely you'll utter hate

Broken Hearted

F**k love!

Love is overrated

I'm tired of the charades

I loved you wholeheartedly, baring every part of me,

every time I let you back, I always get played

Now I use my heartache, play to win, follow suite like a game of spades

Over the years the importance of love has diminished

No one values relationships now, too preoccupied entertaining the critics

People are content being the side piece and unafraid to admit it

For me, to trust anything or anyone would only bewilder, even if I earned top dollar for it

Can't you see I'm conflicted?

Can't you see the essence of my pain?

After all the love I gave, all I craved was to be loved the same.

But love has seared my heart only anguish holds me in

And bars me from devoting myself to love again

Devil in a Red Dress

She has impeccable beauty, smooth skin worn by an amazing frame; she's soft-spoken with seductive game

A deity with most scandalous plots.

The type of woman who'll rip out a man's heart for her feast and toy with it til it rots

Blinding you with her appearance,

she carries herself like a woman should.

Beneath the surface, more than just long hair and pretty eyes, she's damaged and hard as ruby wood

She'll have you mesmerized and keep you in her glowing eyes.

She'll lure you without a touch, tell you what you want to hear; specializing in lies

On a money mission, formulating plans, she's been spiritually; emotionally murdered by many men she carries agony and darkness within

She can reduce a strong man to weak,

and swallow all his pride

she'll engage in conversation, display a little thigh and finesse a man to show and bestow

all he has inside his pockets, turned outside

Look closely; you can see fire in her eyes

Primarily solitary, she has been known to run in packs, usually

first to be noticed, though she parlays way in the back

And by the time a guy approaches she has

planned and in her mind, won her attack

Her scandalous mentality so diabolical,

Her libido is so clever when softly uttered

Intimidated by her presence, most men hope there's a small chance they might stutter, contemplating using a rubber,

she's got you in the palm of her hands,

thinking she likes you, too and utilizes mirror moves on your brother

All I NEED IS YOU

I don't need a model

I don't need a trophy

All I need is you

A woman to laugh with

A loyal woman to come home to

All I need is your love

All I need is your affection

A woman who'll fight for me

All I need is honesty

All I need is truth

A woman who'll love me for me

All I need is you

What sign am I?

I'm a master at being random

One minute you'll love me, the next, you can't stand me

I can be talkative and energetic

Then quiet and distant

My mood can flip in an instant

Be about our business, very persistent

Have you guessed it?

We're not likely to be tested

Unafraid to speak our mind won't shy away from voicing what our minds have detected

Always inconspicuously present

Sometimes forgetful but clearly intelligent

Lovable and such precise etiquette

But if taunts could turn hectic

Cool then dejected

Could go from 0 to 100 in seconds

You'll never know what you'll get dealing with this type of person

If pissed off, talking it out is worthless

Quite perverted

Possess profound ability to adapt in any environment with purpose

Labeling things for what they are, will bring truth to the surface

Clever, witty, charming

Closeness so disarming

Needs space or risk conversion

Curious, impatient, restless

Whatever energy you bring is what you'll receive

Address me in a cool manner and you'll reap the seeds you've conceived

There are some things about women I'll never understand

A woman can have a male friend for 15 years of her life.

He's watched her struggle with different men, consoling her through intense arguments and fights.

He gave her constructive advice informed her there are still good men, but thinking of dating a man and best friend is a sin.

She wouldn't date her friend, but wants her man to be her friend.

There are some things about women I'll never understand.

Her true love could be in her face; she stares at him every day.

Knowing he respects her and has been there for her in every way.

She feels his warmth and grace.

The type of man she prays about when she prays, but emotionally, she won't give him the time of day.

What more does she expect God to do?

What more does a man have to say?

They don't think about the gestures they convey,

still proclaiming there's no good men left and love is so far away.

There are some things about women I'll never understand.

The portrait of a woman

Oh, how I love your pretty face and body

The body of a goddess, you possess such freshly scented aromas in the night, what a sight

The way your jeans hug your curves, how you look in those heels, how, ever so slight, you show your stomach, you pulled it off just right

You're a mighty mustang with seductive sex appeal,

Your conversation is like verbal foreplay, out of succulent lips, glowing eyes and a beautiful smile only an angel can display

Dying Other Half

Writing in tears

I've watched the most crucial person in my life demoralize herself for years

Making drugs nestle her despondency, hoping one day it all disappears

She's slowly killing herself because of emotional distress, her imperfections and her fears

She witnessed her mother and her best friend slaughtered before her eyes and since then her disposition took a downward veer

She can't realize her actions affect everyone spiritually connected to her, displaying I'll always have her rear

I detest that now she's sightless to her self-worth

She's lost a grip on reality, so much misery, so much hurt

I hear her soul scream, like a dream in hell on earth

I've watched her life convert from firm belief in God to not wanting to step foot in a church

Before bed I hear her denounce God, her cries can send chills down your spine begging for her life to revert

Prayer, Faith and God are the way internal healing works

Everyone who professed to love her has dispersed

I try to be strong for her because I know she needs it,

I'll always be there to comfort her

When I pray, I pray that God heals her, that she will lean on Him and anything she wants to know He will reveal to her

It could come in a million different shapes, forms or fashions; I just hope it is in her as her passion

Humane Intentions

As I write these words, making sure my similes curve, assuring every sentence is necessary and true
I draw from the essence of my heart and soul

so whatever I utter I can easily prove

The world needs a model of a person unafraid to broadcast their truths

Celebrating tenacity while prizing human values, I know you've been calculating the steps up to my arrival

Had to reach a decision while perfecting my craft to reveal my title

The personification so vividly clear it's deep rooted in the gifts of a seer

All gestures are sincere with tactics to spread a vital message the masses must hear

We're living for today, we adhere to things no longer near

Holding captive classical views from long gone years

Inside, we're stagnant re-living the past that's not here

A Sinner's Prayer

Dear Lord,

If I die before I wake, I pray to you my soul to take.

Protect me from my foes, closest bros, and those who impose a chameleon face.

Liquidate the impure thoughts that manipulate my black race

Show us a better way.

We say we behave decently, but we live in detrimental ways

Sad to say we've conformed to the artificial nectar, it makes us feel safe

So we've adjusted to its distinctive taste

Living life blindly, knowing deep down it isn't real, that's precisely what makes us fake

Every word is written, every gesture recorded in heaven for display

You endowed us with free will to control our own fate

Oblige us to follow You; guide us to a better place

Soothing the mind

My whole purpose for writing this book was to alleviate your mind, informing people that it's ok to be yourself, to be human

It's ok to be vulnerable, it's ok to cry, it's ok to be wrong, and we'll get more accomplished only if we come together as a unit

We're all going to make mistakes; life sometime causes dismay.

We all have mental melt-downs, it's our perceptions and movements, we depend on if to get to the truth and continue to improve

To attempt to destroy poison pollution

To fumigate our minds, think of clearer solutions

Pardon the intrusion, but I'm tired of losin'

Living in denial is an illusion

Living like you don't do anything wrong only causes more confusion

That twists the mind to believing you're doing what's right when you're totally clueless

My Women

For some strange reason most women TEND to repetitively date the identical type of guy.

Women say good men are difficult to find, when sometimes he may be closer than they realize.

Searching for the bigger prize, falling for the flashy rides while totally ignoring his state of mind.

Failing to recognize that they're searching for a man who's only scripturally inclined

Grasp and understand the fact that there's no such thing as a perfect man, however there is a man perfect for you

You just have to find one worth your time, your loyalty, and who compliments you

Thoroughly evaluating the identity of the man, you give your energy, you or pour out your secrets...

One that's ambitious, self-motivated and brings something to the table

Instead of taking care of a shiftless man when he's so unstable you'll come out better adopting a child or two

Where do you get these men?

You women find them in places the average person wouldn't go

Then you become dumbfounded when you see his true colors show

Till you're labeling all men dirty like bums, the thing about some men is they'll do whatever a woman allows them to do

If you don't require an essential change

Why would you subject yourself to that caliber of pain when you know, in the end your heart may burst into flames?

The walls have eyes

I reside in a divided house; whose silent walls hold captive the echo of voices in the halls and capture all that befalls.

If the walls could talk they'd say there's no love here at all.

In intense squabbles we argue and denounce each other; we're grown and both of us take the fall.

We shoot spit remarks like poison darts of passion, but can't be responsible for our actions.

You have the nerve to get irate with me because it didn't happen the way or when you wanted it to be.

A house can't stand with constant static.

Let's resume love making, our magic, and recall why we first fell in love, even though times are tragic

Let's remain strong when our feelings signal panic

This is the time we have to communicate.

Because this is not a happy home, but there's no other woman I could even imagine being here with me, not one!

Internal truth

As I sleep, open my mind and see me sitting surrounded by darkness and bedlam spiraling from thick marijuana smoke, I clutch two empty beer bottles hoping to relieve my loneliness and liquidate my agony

On cloud 9 and highly intoxicated but the sensation is short-lived and is only mental calamity

There were numerous times I considered suicide

Conversing with the coroner, questioning myself.

Will it even cause a wave if I'm dead or alive?

No one truly loves me anyway; it's all in their eyes

I feel like my flesh has already died.

With a huge daily supply of drugs and alcohol, I feel my spirit float

And feeling paralyzed I'm the result of broken hope

A place where my father was absent, never paid homage

I felt so alone, as though imprisoned, so I remained silent

I knew where he resided, but it's not the same as seeing him when I walked through the door, he shouldn't have HAD to be forced or invited

I can be in a room filled with friends and love ones, but still feel alone and unfound

Pretending to be okay, but my actions seem like me screaming for comfort and guidance

We were supposed to be an alliance

Every waking day I felt those sensations heighten

I often had to laugh to keep from cryin'

Having visions of dying to live life free from stress

Trying to sway and manipulate others I was okay behind my mask so easy to detect

I wish I could lose the thoughts and dilemmas that continue to control me, when the truth is, I need someone to hold me, a sign from God that'll mold me, for my soul needs rest

Ball of Confusion

I don't know whether to let her go or keep her near.

The intimacies we've shared cloud my judgment every time, rendering my decision less and less clear

Like a ball of confusion, not holding control of my next move

is what I most fear

She gets me hard as steel with her perfect oral skills

Seducing my attention, she mesmerizes and I lose focus and become weak-willed

Knowing she's poison of honey brown eyes and a goddess's body

Caught in her trance, completely seduced, I can only kneel

I wage a mental battle with myself, pondering which thoughts to reveal

She has me fully exposed, with more than everything concealed

Her power will not be repealed, nor my sex-drive, while I am the wheel inside the wheel

My mind circles because yes and no both mean yes and leave me frail against her flesh

My wandering eye follows her every move

She constantly captures my interest

But she's detrimental to my body's pure temple

I'm a ball of confusion she bounces and throws, shooting me through delusion

A nice guy gets no credit

Some women will ride and die for a guy that mistreats her,

Uses her, threatens, spiritually defeats her

Yet they remain indebted

But the nice guys receive no credit

He censors her every move

Making her feel like a whore

Accuses her of being used by every dude-she's ever done a favor for

On the other hand, he's planning and perfecting his own methods

While the nice guys always slide into second

She's thinking she can change him

The real him, the profane him

After years of intense fights, unanswered questions, unlearned lessons, she finally gets the message.

From the beginning he should have been emotionally tested

Yet she uproots her emotions for the nice guy while he confides, likewise

nice guys get no credit, but they do get her lies.

I don't respect money

I don't respect money; I respect the hustler's endurance and the methods he exploits to obtain it
Learning how to sustain it
Never committing flagrant acts that jeopardize your morals for monetary gains
Money is the root of all evil; just the love of it can leave you tainted
The love of money will reveal your true character, awakening your truisms, there's no picture you can incorporate to frame it

Exhibiting who you really are, ignorant that the value remains outdated
Risking your freedom all your life to attain it
Is it really worth your body stretched out on the pavement?
Does it tempt you to become cruel and jaded?
Or generous, so you help erase the hatred?
Have you become so complacent after years chasing it?
In the pursuit of self-validation, wondering why your heart is cold and empty
The more they mix color to the dollar, the more its value lessens
Learn to salvage your money, formulate a way to stretch it
The more you crave and lust for it, the more you'll go without finding it

Here we go again

You've crossed my heart with lies before you were forewarned that's the one thing I despise

You possess a face of innocence, but I caught a glimpse of fire in your eyes

Smiles spitting sarcasm while I listen to you stress that you weren't designed to be like those other guys

Standing fast by your side, hoping one day you'd change, but no.

and for all men you've altered my mind's margins

Over and over extending my heart and it's sure to get broken

Been supporting you from the start, but I'm always the one left alone and broken in the dark

Being truthful is where you hesitate, still claiming to love me

Blinded by love, my intuition won't let me sleep, and constantly informs

my heart of what my eyes and I refuse to see

Strengths, Weaknesses and Life Lessons

Chapter 3

Let words be words

Let words be words.
They're not physical touch.
Retaliate when words become verbs; someone who's all about action doesn't talk much.
It's absurd to entertain a man begging to be heard.
When I witness this I think of a furious woman, one who desires much attention.
Usually, when a man is screaming from the top of his lungs he's soft and timid.
Real individuals handle their business without mention.
So evade ignorance, they're only there to stir static and strife.

It's about being smart; one bad decision can destroy your life.
Hear and remember-my words, and apply them to your daily path.
Walk away from misery, to avoid the aftermath.

Soldier's Mentality

You must stand for something or you'll fall for anything

Don't let the ignorance of insolence intervene

Stand and fight for what you believe; remain serene

A soldier's dream

Because if you try having nothing or lack something, strive, live or die.

Your reason for living won't mean a thing

Success

Success entails hard work, isn't preserved for the weak

to become successful, you must compete and when you do, stand all day on your feet

Stand tall, but weep when it's time to weep; in the midst of success you will face shortcomings

Think big, but apply the words that you preach

Success is a conscious decision, down that road you will face slaps and derision and feel you want to breach

Stay where you are; make it happen.

Savor the goals you've worked so hard to reach

Once you've recognized having money isn't just success realizing you'll have to jeopardize not getting enough rest, wanting it more than sleep, more than the air we breathe

Upholding your ambition and drive, not allowing anyone to change your mind, being ready in your eyes is when you'll stand complete

Watch your tongue!!!

Everything isn't meant to be said...

Always think about what you are going to say before you say it.

Choose your words wisely, words are your tool

You don't have to speak every thought moving through your mind; that's the plan of a fool

Understand the power of the tongue; what you utter may shape what your life may become.

Ignorance rests in the bosom of fools who are verbally dumb.

Be mindful of the words you utilize; truth is, you own what you say.

The words you use mark you accountable for your life's outcome.

It would be foolish to denounce God when you who let your mouth run

Uttering the wrong thing may turn and burn you as if you're too close to the sun

You're free to say what you feel but guard yourself at times

Only fools utter everything on their minds

Four Footsteps

As we walk, God walks with us

Knowing our every move, but He gave us free will to let us decide to make it or not

He's always observing, listening to our thoughts and plots

He knows what we're going through and why

He declared his promises to be there when we need Him; He's just waiting till we clearly decide

Whether and if we've had an earthly father, we're all His children through His eyes

He wants to be on our side, displaying truth daily

but some of us do not see that He's the father who's down to provide and

guide us in the right direction but some of us forget to look to the sky

We try to justify our sins; lean on our own understanding, try to convince who brought us into sin we're not living a lie...

We're spiritually dead, if we're not living for the most high

We're functioning corpses til we fully realize; the devil is a lie

He only asked one thing, humble yourself enough to believe and he'll take the lead

all the other commandants and creeds are chores

He will thoroughly screen

We're never alone; that's only what it seems

Just because you can't see wind doesn't mean you can't feel the breeze

Just because you can't see him, doesn't mean he isn't on the scene

Watching over us like owls in trees

He's a loving God and isn't too tough to appease

Calculated steps and with every breath we breathe is witnessed

He displays unconditional love and grace with precision

even through a discreet division

Keep Quiet

If you openly allow people in your love life, they calculate the bounds of your relationship; that could get messy

They may tarnish your relationship, so only resolve your issues behind closed doors, between one another; don't take on needless stressing

You ask why you can't communicate with your spouse because everyone knows what's going on in your house

Don't discuss your relationship struggles with single people

stay quiet as a mouse unless you're sure you have a friend who won't open their mouth

Even then you must be cautious of what comes out

That person you share your dilemmas with, could be the one who'll spread your business about

Remaining quiet may be a more feasible route.

Is Love Enough?

Do I turn left, when nothing is right?

Or do I turn right, when there's nothing left?

It's been eight years and I still haven't made a move

Portraying the fool makes it hard to catch my breath.

Pondering secret plans to be made, avoiding the flashy lights and discriminating cops

The conflicts of love are crossed when sudden immaturity blurred my vision.

One-minute thinking you're going to change, the next you're walking to your old position; ever since, it's causing friction.

It's difficult for me to make a conscious decision to leave, to end the pain addictions

Late night disputes, dawn tensions

Telling coworkers about our hostility

And she wonders why they talk brutality

It's a shame how news beyond your own commutes

And I question myself, "Is love enough?"

It's close to a decade invested in what makes love rough, with nothing to show except true love is honest, but tough

The Characteristics of Love

We want real love and a relationship but refuse the rules it requires

Compromise, sacrifice and understanding all that commitment inflicts.

Most of us are Intolerant, wanting out the moment we're accosted by emotional walls, as if that doesn't come with love

Trying to elevate trust to new heights.

Love is risky it's not 50/50; give your all for life.

What's the point of being open to love, but unwilling to give up your rights?

Actions speak louder than words, whatever befalls; it'll be in plain sight.

No need to retaliate out of spite.

Pay attention, you'll see through the old fables and capers,

some individuals entice.

Stand strong for your love; a real lover would go left to make things right.

So much pain

So much pain but there's so much to gain.

Leaning on our own understanding, thinking we do all right to maintain.

It's a weary mind frame, incapable of framing the main aim.

Patience is vital here in God's domain.

We need Him to eat, we need Him to live, we need His protection

No matter how rich or how high we become

we won't be happy until we realize that God is the only one.

If He wasn't we'd be nothing.

God is our life support when were happy or suffering.

If we seek Him with diligence, we'll see His

Use and see through all the pain and frustration to seek and find God with dedication.

The fear of love

The fear of love is its unexpected anguish

Real love won't create conditions or intermissions despite the rage it unleashes and the chaos in between.

Love is meant to pacify one's spleen, to bring joy and excitement to one's loving dreams

Love obliges us to see completely through things.

To see life is nothing without the pure air love brings

Life would be unlived without love; love would not be without life

Sometimes love inflicts sorrow and pain; love's authenticity is worth fighting love to have life

Embrace your human side

I embrace my truths, weaknesses and flaws.

They make me who I am overall

Not afraid to speak truth, even if truth's embarrassing to do,

Laugh at me but you can't destroy what arose from the root

What surpasses the limits?

Simply confessing makes room for improvement; I confess to reprove my detractors and critics

Unafraid of embarrassment, you can't dispute truth's pure lyrics

Lying furthers the distance between you and truth

Submission to truth reduces liars' intrusions

Words from a Changed Man

Trying to keep my head above water.

It's hard as hell to take care of a family, without being taught.

Truthfully, I do get distraught

Luckily for me, I have a wife who supports me, who's there for me

when my thoughts turn ugly and turn me around

I balk about letting them down.

I won't quit, but only press on.

Doing what I got to do for my wife and kids for them to have food to eat, clothes on their backs and cozy beds for them to rest on.

I'm always facing it head on.

Trusting God will have my back when things go wrong.

Leading my family strong

I had to lose my selfish need for what's mine; a house divided has no spine

I've learned, when you work as a team, having each other's backs

that's how you make a house into your happy home

Tired of running...

Tired of running from my past...

Tired of running from what I feel...

Tired of running from the truth...

Tired of running from what's real...

Tired of running from my sorrow...

Tired of running from the pain...

I've come to realize I've been running from myself

Seems I've lost my primary aim

Attempting to grasp monetary gain

Seems I've lost my picture frame

As if just avoiding the rain

When I need to

To obliterate the riots flowing, racing, through my brain, I must confront all my fears struggle to attain contentment

Good morning

As I wake up, yawning and wiping the crust out my eyes

I hope and pray I have a good day

I get up and go outside to see the sun shining, hear the birds chirping

I stretch my arms out and look up at the clear blue sky

I start to pray for myself, my family, and anyone who's hurting

How your morning begins is how your day may end

Don't let anyone ruin your joy for the day

Some people never have anything good to say

In case they do have something to say

Murder them with kindness; turn to tell them good morning and have a nice day

Cherish a good woman

You'll be amazed at how understanding a woman can be when she truly loves you.

In all honesty, they take a lot of shit from us, knowingly and unknowingly,

Amazing isn't it?

Taking you back after cheating, being sneaky fracturing her trust, that's almost equivalent to God's kind of love

So, fostering a good woman is a must.

Smooth Operator

Whenever approaching a woman all she can say is yay or nay

Why utilize profanity with letters beginning with B and H, all because you didn't get your way

No matter what you say

You were attracted to her if she's stuck up or just having a tiresome day

Always conclude the conversation with "Have a blessed day."

She'll never forget your face because it's something she may not be used to

No matter what they say

Women are emotional creatures, the trick is to cause a chilling sensation down her spine, and she has to feel the words you illustrate

You could possibly modify her decision depending on the choice of words you articulate

I'm the type of guy that sits humbly in the cut, witnessing all the men hover around the woman,

Five men accosting her; she's already defensive, maybe even apprehensive but she remains passive to their self-made genius

For just one of them to obtain her number is slim chance; I don't want to be near that vicinity

Women breed curiosity and that creates possibilities

Grown minded women respond to power, confidence, and common sense,
not nothing flashy or a man's desperate, dry-mouthed terminology

She sees through them like glass,

all eyes on me pondering what I'm thinking

why I'm the only one paying no attention to her and her disdain for biology

Be a man to your woman

A woman doesn't want a man she can push around.

She wants a man to be a man, one who can boldly stand his ground

Be a man not a mouse

At times when she's attempting to sway the situation put your foot down and boldly open your mouth

Declare your verdict!

Women were bred to comply with her man's expressions; if she loves and trusts you she'll always follow your route

It'll require mere diligence, exhibiting love with consistence, but on the contrary, be dominant.

Don't face her with timidity, with all that whispering put some bass in your voice and maybe she won't mind listening

Ladies, respect yourself

Ladies, reframe from opening your legs before setting your criteria first

Know who you're with before you call yourself loving them because you may lead your emotions in a mental hurst

Know your worth; mind the inclinations and messages you send

All women should be appreciated with a passion, but how do you expect men or anybody to respect you if you don't respect yourself first?

Respect is earned not given

Thirsty for attention, got men staring, squishing their leers looking through your clear skirt

Every time they see you, whatever they've witnessed last is what they'll be thinking out of thirst

Showcase your intellect and watch how swiftly the conversation converts

Some men can't even converse

Some men are intimidated by an intelligent woman's perks

That's just the way some men's minds function

This should be read out loud, laid back, while your friends are around your ready crossroads

Be cautious of things you do if you want a man who'll respect you

If you didn't dress like you're exploiting sex,

perhaps some men wouldn't approach you

Calling you out your name if you weren't dressed in degrading context

Love and respect yourself and respect will come your way

It's more about how you're perceived than the words you say

No longer blind

I was blinded to her inability to commit and be faithful

You were my precious angel

Even when we didn't have a label, there were moments I wasn't working, yet I made sure I brought something to the table

I did almost anything you asked of me; even after a tragedy

I performed when I was physically unable

In return, all I asked from you was a covenant, your loyalty to your family, and your judgment

The kids didn't ask for this, nor did they deserve this mental torment

I thought this is what you wanted, a man that not only talks, but also shows his love for his woman

I guess you've been yearning for it so long, but were stopped by the guys who didn't come home at a decent time; it frightens you to know a good man

You've shown me, without doubt, that's something you can't stand

So, I've contrived a plan of letting go of your hand

You're thinking you can play me when I'm cool as a fan

Thinking you're slicker than oil when I sculpted the can

Your constant critiquing its design and the way it stands

I see through your cunning gestures and spiteful plans

You'll realize there's none like me, I'm a far better quality of man

My Love

My love flows deep like the sea

Tightly holds your body captive, calm and refreshing, an awakening from a long night of sleep

It captures you, surrounds you, until no aspect of your body is seen

Yet I am sensitive to trusting; as long as you're loyal, I would spend time and money on my lady

Giving you the time you need

Confessing my love for you 'til you spiritually leave

Spiritually joined by the mind and body, I'll broadcast my love for you

Before anybody

Our love can transcend to a pinnacle no man can reach

A bond of our caliber, so powerful no man can breach

Exhibiting love only a real man can teach

Just be there, hold me down when distractions arise

Be the one who wakes in the morning and I will attend to everything else left undone

Forgive Me

Forgive me; I'm the one to blame for proclaiming infliction of your pain

When will I ever see you smile again?

How could I allow a perfect love to turn so blain?

Relentless, I hurt you and watched your self-esteem evaporate like a rainbow after a rain

I never meant to become so profane, yet again

Whenever I needed you, you were there to help me make repairs

I made things worse even after they had grown bad

Although immature, my reactions came with hopes you'd feel the fire pulsing through my veins

But it backfired; there were nothing left to hope or to gain

The impact of that reaction was that I felt stupid, even insane in my own domain

You weren't the cause of my agony; I could not manage the struggle we bore financially.

It was stressful, so I began to sabotage with scorn but that caused heavy heartbreak and shared disaster

I can't stand looking in your eyes, knowing I've failed you, I made you cry

For that, I sincerely apologize

This comes from my heart, not like before, time and again, when I tried to persuade you to believe a lie

Afterwards I always felt guilt inside

Even so, you were my angel under my wing

All I ever wanted was to see you emerge and fly

I didn't want our relationship to end but in the midst of it my pride overcame making amends

Just like most men, we realize at the end

I was fortunate to have had you; it was a privilege to say I knew you.

Forgive my transgressions, my love, for you were forever

but I allowed my pride to turn that to never

I hate that I've allowed my immaturity to crush our future plans

I didn't want that at all; I should have been more of a man

Keep your eyes and ears open

Sometimes everything isn't what it seems

Everything that glistens and gleams isn't always supreme

Human eyes can be deceived and become deceiving

Obtain knowledge before you begin believing

A man who stands for nothing will fall for anything

It may sound intriguing, but it doesn't mean it's the rightful dream

Like deer in fast, bright, oncoming headlights, we are blinded by the still brighter beams...

Read between the lines cause there's always a price, an impact that follows the schemes

Sometimes we are mistaken and fooled by the looks of things

Choices

Life or death

Money or wisdom

God or Satan

Which will you choose to resolve your enigma?

Will you keep doing the same or will you cite a better aim

There's life or death in your tongue so don't complain when things don't get redone

Life is what you make it; there's only yourself to blame

Some of us choose darkness, living life heartless, believing it's all just a game

From the first, our souls glory in heaven, not being swallowed by flames

Everything you see is temporary, the real truth is unseen

Cleanse your brain of all misconceptions; don't drown in the seas of deception

And you will be in the right lane when you make your connection

I'm only stating facts and bestowing suggestions

God already declared His promise

Come judgment day, there'll be no clemency, just playbacks without exceptions

Some things in life are simply unavoidable

There are just some things in life that are unavoidable

Like haters, cowards, or people who are disloyal

Let them continue to hate.

Let them continue to talk.

Let them continue to be fake.

Regardless of what you say, in their hearts they'll stay the same way.

It's nothing you can do or say to make them look worse than their own actions portray

Be observant to the gestures individuals convey.

Learn to stay away

The people who anger you control you

Real G's move in silence; worry not about who's real or fake

Only you can control you and all you say

Why we broke up

We broke up because all she wanted was to participate in emotional games,
all I wanted was assurance to elucidate; she wasn't able to reciprocate...
Unfortunately, that's where we often clashed
Deeply yearning for our harmony to elevate
We were supposed to fumigate the toxic waste, to restore, regenerate,
Thinking things will revert, falling back to their original state...
Hoping that it would last, knowing it would surely deflate

We've permitted distractions bar us from reaching a higher state,

focusing too much on the past until now when it's too late
We're grown adults. I felt like we could repair any problem; there were some things I felt I shouldn't have to reiterate
I sensed I would endure some negative backlash
So old habits I would gradually break and obliterate
Every time one dissolved, I witnessed a constant flash
Exposing things so hard, we should have begun to communicate
Agreeing to disagree, and with lingering problems, we should've tried to eliminate

Anticipating the moment, we pushed forward to spiritually elevate
When we aren't in each other's face, we thoughtlessly denigrate each other's names
When we were in each other's presence there were the fables immaturity could not validate
Attempting to pick each other's mental stash did not allow us to elaborate
So preoccupied trying to educate, at the same time trying to manipulate
In the beginning I would've braved an earthquake to stay

Sometimes we want so much to build on a bond with a person; that same bond God could've been trying to separate

Mistakes

Mistakes are going to be made

How do you expect to advance as a man if you can't realize a mistake has been conveyed?

We're so quick to broadcast or expose another person's flaws

Yet you can't account for none of yours at all

It takes a man to know when he's wrong; it takes a bigger man to learn after he falls

We're entitled to screw up

The word good is a human lie

Quick to condemn, we lack judgement of what lies behind our own eye

What you won't do, another man will

Fellas, take good care of your woman because what you won't do another man won't hesitate

If she's beautiful, loyal and the love is authentic, what's the point of cheating?

If she took care of you in the midst of a drought and you can trust her without doubt, what's the point of leaving?

We are all well-aware of how complex it is to locate someone decent and true.

Someone who'll be there no matter what, who'll love you for you.

If you already have a Ferrari, why would you trade it for a Lincoln?

The grass isn't always greener on the other side,

The years and energy invested in a relationship aren't worth losing for one fun-filled weekend.

Respect the value of your woman cause if she's a good one, the one you're creepin' with could be creepin'.

4Giveness

We must learn to forgive and in the process, forgive ourselves

To grow we must make mature decisions

To excel we must mirror forgiveness to be forgiven,

To conquer fear of submission, to be free from unresolved hate.

You don't always forgive for them, sometimes you forgive for you

Develop your sense of betterment to deepen the character within you

Holding on to grudges, unable to grasp why your plans are often discontinued

Feeling stagnant, living in the past, and confused, you're looking up and down a menu without hunger

They say it's easy to forgive someone you don't know, but try forgiving someone you love

We must forgive to be forgivable

So, forgive and allow the venom to seep away til it's invisible

Real Life

Chapter 4

Self-Respect

Why does it seem I'm witnessing more and more black women respond rapidly to Bitch, Hoe, Shorty or Yo?

In one day I've witnessed it eight times in a row

Are those the only words they know how to respond to?

Why does it have to sound corny or comical when daring to be original?

They'll place the nice guy in a cubicle, content being degraded, hearing every word but beautiful

Why? Because it sounds like game!

If you are beautiful why does it sound insane?

Perhaps it's just my environment, or their minds were molded into refusal to change

How can a decent man compete with words that degrade?

Labeling yourself a bitch?

Pay attention to the clues and messages you're sending

If you refer to yourself as a bitch, there's no self-respect, there was none from the start

To be respected you must first respect yourself

To label yourself what you don't want to take from a man conveys no help

The proclaim to want respect, but leave their dignity and self-respect on the shelf

Give a man something to respect instead of something to neglect.

Not every man will fall weak just because you're showing your ass and chest.

Don't get the wrong idea; it looks very appealing, but there's a time and place for sex.

Some men yearn for women of standards, with self-respect

Other women search everywhere, always desperate for a man with a check.

Loud Ones

Loud dudes only want attention, but beware of the quiet ones because their less mentioned.

You'll be difficult to locate if your body comes up missin`.

Dude always feel like they have to display their masculinity, when they're really masking their sensitivity.

Rather than being men they're attention whores.

True men's power is calm self-control

Loner

I know that feeling when it feels like nobody care.

When you're going through your problems seems like nobody there.

Over the years I've learned having too many friends can be an obstacle to future plans; everyone around you is not a fan,

Shameless thoughts swim through my brain; there's no one to vent to, except to vent in pain and in vain

The more you expose yourself the more your state turns critical

The less you talk the fewer your chances of becoming statistical

Although consumed by loneliness

It is an illusion to have someone to reveal my dilemmas and delusions

I don't have many friends, so poetry became a substitute,

I write to release signals, because it's unbearable for me to trust individuals

I got it bad

I'm a loner, so some say I'm anti-social; I ostracize, refuse to socialize with any females or guys who ooze strange energy and vibes

Not the gregarious type, very skeptical about with whom I talk or chill; some people are devils in disguise

I'm only accompanied by real individuals who reject all drama or negativity, who embody self-growth and cut off all profanity without gain or ties

I consider the friends I do have as family; that's where my loyalty lies

Been there since the beginning of time.

Whenever I needed them, there was never a problem to show up where I reside

If it's apparent I'm uncomfortable and I don't converse, don't be surprised

I'm one of those loner guys whose silence is strength, despite a closed mouth and opened eyes

I know my position

I'm a man who knows his position, will never switch or merge lanes

I'm real with myself so in any environment I can adapt and survive

Being respected, born with an honorable name

Trying to live up to it, highly favored so I can't complain

Concentrating on my goals, breaking down barriers, with my family and comrades who motivate and stand behind me like unseen, powerful carriers

Standing tall like a monument, making sure to stay prayed up, trying not to go back to old habits

Following the path God has set for me, watching things come together like magnets

The more I'm obedient to God's word, the more it protects me from becoming stagnant

Staying strong, having the right people around, in my home, respecting things I don't condone, good folks around keep me from traps of chaos and static

Still aren't satisfied

You say you don't want a broke, lazy man, but you want a man to stay at home all day with you

Complaining that your man has no ambition, no drive or no goals to derive

But when that's all changed, you still aren't satisfied

When you're cold and alone, you ask another man home on those nights to hold you

Knowing you have a committed man who'll go thru hell and high water for you

Keeping the covenant, you both agreed to, love, honor and respect,

He works hard to make money to take good care of you.

But when he recommends that you seek employment, you misjudge, thinking he's trying to control you

The truth is, he's trying to show you that working as a team means no one will come before you

Ladies, if you want a man to be at home with you all the time, be prepared to struggle

If you want a hardworking man who does all he can to secure you,

guy's future plans, learn patience, seek something else for comfort,

he's doing his job; try not to make it hard,

if you're uncomfortable with the job he's doing find some other life to ruin.

Been waiting on your love

It's beyond physical; I love you from my soul

Loving you to death, but these arguments are out of control

It's as if you like to see me angry, being all exposed…

When my trust is what I've gladly let you hold

Sick of this scandalous shit I deal with, it takes every inch of my energy not to explode.

Pressing my buttons, knowing I won't hit you, but you quick to utter you don't care, you're not afraid to let it all go.

Tell me what is a man to do when all he wants is to feel loved and believe in you?

Rather than fighting me, fighting for me is what you need to do.

Everything I do, I do for me and you, but for you, always on purpose, to fix your lips to be slick is disrespectful, it's pushing me away, I'm swimming in thoughts of being single

Where I can mingle and be with a woman who can love me, tired of waiting on a woman to learn how to love me and not be so evil

You couldn't possibly know how deep this pain runs or how it feels

I've wasted eight years of my life waiting on you to yield

Enduring your cunning remarks like throwing darts at my heart, I would start to think you did it for your own personal thrill

Using my body as a human shield all these years, trying to protect you from damn near everything, instead of protecting the emotions I feel

They say when you really love a person like I love you, you must let them go, but I hate to see you cry

Either make an effort to change or it's time to say goodbye

Tired Of Being Tired

Tired of the arguments, the intense disputes

Won't settle for it any longer, the yelling and cursing should have been my cues

In the beginning, everything was beautiful, like when you first opened your eyes to witness the sun rise

But now you intentionally taunt me, in my ear, following me to witness what I'm really capable of

I know a lot of men who abuse their woman but I just can't put my hands on the woman I love and you know that and you use it to your advantage

Just extremely annoyed with this entire situation

Leaving you is long overdue and outdated

I'll be happier and focused by myself minus the drama

Trying to appease you with love, attention and gifts, it's never enough.

Tired of making mere gestures I thought were the correct things to do,

but nothing seems to satisfy you, nothing seems to be right

And wonder why I can't sleep peacefully some nights?

You want me to make some of what you call "necessary modifications."

But continuously accuse me of these unrealistic allegations

I work hard every day, make sure you are good, so I think I deserve to come home to a loving girlfriend but I'm the one who always has to be patient

Love doesn't come with conditions but how long do you expect me to continue waiting?

Playing the role of a parole officer putting me under surveillance and intense interrogations

I've been giving you the benefit of the doubt, knowing that's not you at all,

Trying to make you look good in front of people I know, who surely don't like you

You'd rather believe a premeditated lie than the simple truth

I don't know how much longer I can endure this mental and physical abuse from a woman that's not putting her love for me to use

I've not only said I love you but I've displayed it too, anything I've uttered I can at least show and prove.

Like doing things in this relationship that in my past relationships I normally wouldn't do; buying the clothes, the shoes, food and pay the bills, and the fact that you compensate for nothing and I'm working hard to take care of the both of us

Tired of demonstrating and expressing that everything I do, I do

for me and you but you stressing me, when I've been truly faithful to you

You proceed to slander men names like you have a bad one. Allowing your hating ass, forever single ass friends influence you to speak that way

I've tried being understanding and considerate to the fact that your last man hurt you and the past could be difficult to erase.

I've been here this long, I work hard, I love you and I show you as I stand directly in your face

It's time to pay attention and take responsibility for your actions, yes, you've been hurt before but no man has dominion over the way you behave and the things you say

Only you possess power over you and the actions you portray

You're treating me how your previous man treated you.

You say men are dogs.

You have the nerve to ask that question: "How could any man cheat on me?" Look how you treated me.

I don't know how long this will last but I'm tired of you accusing me, the constant sarcasm and the influence that your lonely ass friends have on you and someone's actions from your past

Continue and you will lose the man you claim you truly love

I don't expect you to be perfect but for us to move forward all of this nonsense, fake friends and past relationships drama must be discarded immediately.

Life Is Precious

Start cherishing life today

The most pivotal events in life are those that take your breath away

Shun negativity in order to excel

Surround yourself with people who are about advancement, who are self-motivated, who want to see you win

Watch who you hang out with; "Birds of a feather flock together"

By the company you keep you can stand the backlash of their actions

One wrong mishap, you could spend the rest of your life in jail

Being told when to eat, when to sleep with two or more men crammed in one cell?

Another form of hell.

Life is what you make it; you could live wisely and well, or continue making it harder to exhale

Success is proof you refused to become another statistic and fail

Make an effort; if you never try, how will you ever know if you'll find your internal treasure

It's more than being clever, life is precious; we should cherish it together

Faith without works is dead

Read between the lines

When we pray for patience…

God doesn't grant patience, He gives us a chance to gain patience

Try to see it through His eyes

When we pray for courage…

God doesn't grant courage, He places us in situations to see if we become courageous.

He endows us with free will, the potential to control our own fate

Faith without works is dead

We have to utilize the right words, ask the right questions, according to which direction our prayers were led

Act on His time to get ahead

Everything is already written; we just have to remind Him of the promises He said

Fears

I'm man enough to admit and say... I'm afraid, afraid to give my love away

It's hard for me to trust anyone or anything; doing so has driven me into an empty place

I'm tense and the intensity grows by the minute, develops rapidly like children,

Viciously venting, maybe breaking my own covenant, not intentionally, nor to destroy, but my pride usually does it

Sabotaging my love because I'm petrified to submit

My trust issues stop me; I cannot fully commit

Existing in a world where I see such unfaithfulness

Some say I'm too emotionally stalled

I say love has too many emotions involved

When a relationship is damaged, it strains to evolve

Like when you're too deep, being deep in the streets, when money rules overall

The situation grows hectic; it becomes complicated to see or escape, having visions I want to eliminate

Seems as soon as you utilize the word love, the quicker it'll be a way to replace or be replaced

We're living in times when it's acceptable to have a side piece, so I refuse to look love in its face

My Mission

My main mission is to be more than just a poetic descendant

To venture on to other avenues, to excel past what I've first envisioned

Making investments, giving people jobs, and opening up businesses

While simultaneously suggesting changes to the ways we've been livin'

Becoming a better man, implementing my plans, teaching elevation and restoration to cut the hatred birthed from my statements if I can make them listen

Being a blessing to people's lives, obliging people, putting smiles on people's faces, bringing forth change to a person's life are my deepest intentions

With my words I hope to heal old wounds and lacerations

We're so preoccupied with our own lives and how we're livin' that it doesn't help anyone and that's what we're forgettin'

It's about accommodating one another, unifying so we can bless a person, putting them in a better financial position.

Demonstrating love without being mentioned Truth without condition

Congregating against all odds but with good intentions, let's learn to love one another as well as ourselves; life is much easier when there's less tension

Goodbye

Saying goodbye is one of the hardest things to do
Especially when you genuinely love and care for a person, and know we simply aren't compatible
When you know the situation just isn't right, it's mandatory that it has to be done
Or you'll find yourself settling, unhappy with the wrong one
Remaining planted because you're comfortable, while allowing true love to continue to shun
The love may be there, but it isn't fair to deprive yourself of real love.
I've tried everything I can think of, but after 8 years I've totally ignored the signs from above
Your heart I attempted to seize but you're impossible to appease
Saying it's the little things that count, only made your actions show you were displeased
Reminding you of the words you've once uttered but you always act as though I'm speaking Chinese
Always in the club and in the streets being a sleaze but you wonder why when you say you love me it's beyond possible to believe
On the contrary, not wanting to start over, I found comfort while feeling uncomfortable
Wanting to excel and move forward, starting a decent family that's indestructible, modeled like the Huxtables
In the beginning, I was naive to think, as a couple, we were untouchable
We clearly aren't meant for each other; our relationship became extremely dysfunctional

Blindfolded

Steadily ignoring decent men for these phony mask men.

Haven't altered your ways, but continue to date the same type of men, thinking you've caught a better package.

No doubt driven by attraction, hoping for sexual satisfaction and it's got you draggin'

5 + 15 equals 20, but so does 14 + 6, it's just simple mathematics…

You think going about it in a different way might get a different reaction.

It's the sneaky tactics you were bypassin', the true questions you weren't askin' that have left you lackin'

Perhaps it's your own actions that allow love to continue passin'

Lies (The reason why men lie)

Most dudes feel it's more preferable to tell the truth, but the reason why we lie is not because we wish to hurt you,

It's the backlash of the reaction we wish to elude

First of all, everybody lies, big lies, small lies, white lies, a ruse, lying with your actions

It's still a lie; they're all under the same label

A lie doesn't care who expresses it, or whether or not we're all capable of telling one

Sometimes the truth is just too much to digest and too simple to believe

If you're ill-tempered, some would rather lie than leave,

sweetening up the tangled web they continue to weave

We are what we think

I will repeatedly say that we were meant to shine

But nothing comes easy

We must renew our minds

Refusing to allow ignorance to bar us from our primary goal, to keep us from reaching financial advancement

In the pursuit of happiness, practicing what we preach,

Speaking things, we desire into existence, working hard to see what we've claimed

We are what we think, we have what we say, there's power in the tongue

The only way for things to change is if we alter the wicked thoughts and gestures we convey

Making up methods like entrepreneurs instead of just living for the day

It's time to begin using our brains; the information is inside them for all we wish to create

We've had enough breaks.

The longer we delay the change, the longer it'll take us to correct our errors, then to elevate

Author Samuel Donte Djuan Davis

Described as a very reserved kid...

Author Samuel Donte Djuan Davis born in Gary, IN and raised in Atlanta, GA raised in the church and sung in the choir, he was never one to follow others he moved by the beat of his own drum. A fast learner, things came to him rather easy and he excelled in most things that he put his determined mind to and led by example. His peers respected him for standing his ground and living his life moral based, he was willing to try anything once in his youth, but was quick to realize what was for him and not for him. He used his sense of reasoning and maturity in his youth wisely to avoid the pitfall that most of his peers could not, selling drugs, getting locked up, staying in trouble, he managed to escape the ever-present threats. He grew up in an environment that had all of the ills of the world and somehow kept himself on the straight and narrow. The saying "Birds of a Feather Flock Together" was always close in his mind of reasoning, he knew that just by association he could be found guilty of a crime in court or in the eyes of the public so he stuck to his moral compass to guide him thru his young youth and it served him well. He encountered opposition to his way of thinking at every turn, fighting daily peer pressure and stereotypical views from the surrounding public, and he still pressed on determined to do great things in his life.

Samuel knew that he wanted to share his many gifts with the world, so he found himself one day talking to himself; he wondered which one of his many gifts would he share with the world, who will listen if he spoke, and will it be of any value. He asked God "reveal to me my talent that I can share with the world", then and there he knew that his gift of expression would be what God wanted him to share with the world. Samuel also knew that this very thing would be the catalyst of change in his and his family's' lives, his words of expression would make a difference. He delivers his first of many gifts Human Intentions Vol. 1 a collection of thought provoking poems with a wide range of influences which dives into the conversations of what both men and women have on their hearts and minds. Samuel brings you into his world and shares with you various ways of thoughts, feelings, perspectives, moods and lessons learned growing up from a youth to a man.

www.ingramcontent.com/pod-product-compliance
Lightning Source LLC
Chambersburg PA
CBHW060419010526
44118CB00017B/2277